Tar Heelology Trivia Challenge

North Carolina Tar Heels Basketball

Tar Heelology Trivia Challenge – North Carolina Tar Heels Basketball;
Third Edition 2008

Published by
Kick The Ball, Ltd
8595 Columbus Pike, Suite 197
Lewis Center, OH 43035
www.TriviaGameBooks.com

Designed, Formatted, and Edited by: Paul F. Wilson & Tom P. Rippey III
Researched by: Paul F. Wilson

*For information on ordering this book in bulk at reduced prices, please email us
at pfwilson@trivianthology.com.*

International Standard Book Number: 978-1-934372-27-2

Printed & Bound in the United States of America

Paul F. Wilson & Tom P. Rippey III

Tar Heelology Trivia Challenge

North Carolina Tar Heels Basketball

Researched by Paul F. Wilson

Paul F. Wilson & Tom P. Rippey III, Editors

Kick The Ball, Ltd
Lewis Center, Ohio

iii

This book is dedicated to our families and friends for your unwavering love, support, and your understanding of our pursuit of our passions. Thank you for everything you do for us and for making our lives complete.

Dear Friend,

Thank you for purchasing our *Tar Heelology Trivia Challenge* game book!

We hope you enjoy it as much as we enjoyed researching and putting it together. This book can be used over and over again in many different ways. One example would be to use it in a head-to-head challenge by alternating questions between Tar Heel basketball fans – or by playing as teams. Another option would be to simply challenge yourself to see how many questions you could answer correctly. No matter how you choose to use this book, you'll have fun and maybe even learn a fact or two about Tar Heels basketball.

We have made every attempt to verify the accuracy of the questions and answers contained in this book. However it is still possible that from time to time an error has been made by us or our researchers. In the event you find a question or answer that is questionable or inaccurate, we ask for your understanding and thank you for bringing it to our attention so that we may improve future editions of this book. Please email us at tprippey@trivianthology.com with those observations and comments.

Have fun playing *Tar Heelology Trivia Challenge*!

Paul & Tom

Paul Wilson & Tom Rippey
Co-Founders, Kick The Ball, Ltd

PS – You can discover more about all of our current trivia game books by visiting us online at www.TriviaGameBooks.com.

Table of Contents

How to Play

Book Format:

There are four quarters, each made up of fifty questions. Each quarter's questions have assigned point values. Questions are designed to get progressively more difficult as you proceed through each quarter, as well as through the book itself. Most questions are in a four-option multiple-choice format so that you will at least have a 25% chance of getting a correct answer for some of the more challenging questions.

We've even added an *Overtime* section in the event of a tie, or just in case you want to keep playing a little longer.

Game Options:

One Player -
To play on your own, simply answer each of the questions in all the quarters, and in the overtime section, if you'd like. Use the *Player / Team Score Sheet* to record your answers and the quarter *Answer Keys* to check your answers. Calculate each quarter's points and the total for the game at the bottom of the *Player / Team Score Sheet* to determine your final score.

Two or More Players –
To play with multiple players decide if you will all be competing with each other individually, or if you will form and play as teams. Each player / team will then have its own *Player / Team Score Sheet* to record its answer. You can use the quarter *Answer Keys* to check your answers and to calculate your final scores.

1

The *Player / Team Score Sheets* have been designed so that each team can answer all questions or you can divide the questions up in any combination you would prefer. For example, you may want to alternate questions if two players are playing or answer every third question for three players, etc. In any case, simply record your response to your questions in the corresponding quarter and question number on the *Player / Team Score Sheet*.

A winner will be determined by multiplying the total number of correct answers for each quarter by the point value per quarter, then adding together the final total for all quarters combined. Play the game again and again by alternating the questions that your team is assigned so that you will answer a different set of questions each time you play.

You Create the Game -
There are countless other ways of using **Tar Heelology Trivia Challenge** questions. It's limited only to your imagination. Examples might be using them at your tailgate or other college basketball related party. Players / Teams who answer questions incorrectly may have to perform a required action, or winners may receive special prizes. Let us know what other games you come up with!

Have fun!

1) What is the name of the Tar Heels' current home arena?

    A) Roy Williams Center
    B) Carmichael Auditorium
    C) Dean E. Smith Center
    D) Woollen Gym

2) By which other name is the officially licensed "Carolina Blue" also known?

    A) Columbia Blue
    B) Baby Blue
    C) Powder Blue
    D) Light Blue

3) In which Conference do the Tar Heels play?

    A) Southeastern Conference
    B) Atlantic Coast Conference
    C) Sun Belt Conference
    D) Conference USA

4) Which of the following ACC opponents is considered the Tar Heels' biggest historic rival?

    A) Miami
    B) Georgia Tech
    C) Virginia
    D) Duke

5) The University of North Carolina is located in which city?

    A) Charlotte
    B) Wilmington
    C) Chapel Hill
    D) Mount Cathedral

6) What is the name of North Carolina's Alma Mater?

    A) Here Comes Carolina
    B) Hark The Sound
    C) Tar Heels on Hand
    D) Carolina Victory

7) The Tar Heels have greater than 1,900 all-time team victories.

    A) True
    B) False

8) What is the Tar Heels' mascot's name?

    A) Battering Ram
    B) Woollen's Ram
    C) Huggin's Ram
    D) Rameses the Ram

9) What is the famous offensive set created by Coach Smith in 1965?

A) Three-Corners
B) Four-Corners
C) Triangle
D) The Box

10) In which year was the first game played in the Smith Center?

A) 1983
B) 1984
C) 1985
D) 1986

11) How many NCAA Titles have the Tar Heels won?

A) 2
B) 3
C) 4
D) 5

12) Who is the Tar Heels' current head coach?

A) Roy Williams
B) Frank McGuire
C) Bill Guthridge
D) Dean Smith

13) In the 1999-2000 season the "North Carolina" lettering on the front of the Tar Heels' uniforms was replaced with what?

A) "UNC" Abbreviation
B) Interlocking "NC" logo
C) Interlocking "TH" logo
D) "Tar Heels"

14) In 1982 Michael Jordan's 17' championship-winning jump shot was over which team?

A) Michigan
B) Illinois
C) Kansas
D) Georgetown

15) By what other name is the Tar Heels' Educational Foundation known?

A) Rams Club
B) Heels for Higher Education
C) Heels for Scholarship & Athletics
D) Rameses Club

16) Do the Tar Heels retire players' jersey numbers?

A) Yes
B) No

17) Including the Tar Heels, how many teams comprise the ACC?

   A) 8
   B) 10
   C) 12
   D) 14

18) What is the origin of the nickname Tar Heels?

   A) Ship that brought the earliest NC settlers
   B) Unknown
   C) Shoes were one of the state's early products
   D) Tar taken from forests for the English Navy

19) James Worthy, Sam Perkins, and Michael Jordan were all named First Team Consensus All-American in the same season.

   A) True
   B) False

20) How many all-time NCAA Tournament appearances have the Tar Heels had?

   A) 31
   B) 40
   C) 42
   D) 44

Preseason

21) Former Tar Heel Vince Carter was drafted by which team in the First Round of the NBA Draft?

    A) Chicago Bulls
    B) Toronto Raptors
    C) Golden State Warriors
    D) New Jersey Nets

22) Tar Heels coach Bill Guthridge does not hold the D-1 Best Career Starts by Wins record for one season.

    A) True
    B) False

23) Tar Heel great Brad Daugherty was selected first overall in the 1986 NBA Draft by which team?

    A) Denver Nuggets
    B) Utah Jazz
    C) Cleveland Cavaliers
    D) Detroit Pistons

24) How many times was Tar Heel Eric Montross selected Second Team Consensus All-American?

    A) 0
    B) 2
    C) 3
    D) 4

25) Coach Dean Smith was born in which state?

    A) Kansas
    B) Missouri
    C) Iowa
    D) Nebraska

26) How many players did the Tar Heels have on the ACC 50th Anniversary Team?

    A) 5
    B) 7
    C) 9
    D) 12

27) The Tar Heels have had 92 players selected in the NBA Draft.

    A) True
    B) False

28) Which of the following Tar Heels was not named Most Outstanding Player of the Final Four?

    A) Sean May
    B) James Worthy
    C) Donald Williams
    D) Antawn Jamison

29) How many regular-season ACC Championships have the Tar Heels won?

    A) 26
    B) 28
    C) 30
    D) 32

30) UNC set a team record for the most Personal Fouls (36) in an NCAA Tournament game against which team?

    A) Texas A&M
    B) Louisville
    C) Georgia
    D) UCLA

31) UNC has 67 all-time All-ACC First Team selections, which team is second with 57?

    A) Maryland
    B) Virginia
    C) Clemson
    D) Duke

32) Which of these Tar Heels was not a four-year starter?

    A) Phil Ford
    B) Kenny Smith
    C) Jeff Lebo
    D) Vince Carter

33) The Tar Heels have greater than 500 all-time ACC wins.

    A) True
    B) False

34) How many coaches and players do the Tar Heels have in the Basketball Hall of Fame?

    A) 5
    B) 6
    C) 8
    D) 9

35) How many Tar Heels have scored 1,000 or more points in their college career?

    A) 59
    B) 69
    C) 79
    D) None of the above

36) Against which team did the Tar Heels play their very first game?

    A) Lynchburg YMCA
    B) Virginia Christian
    C) NC State
    D) Mississippi State

37) What is the Tar Heels' team record for most consecutive NCAA Tournament appearances?

    A) 26
    B) 27
    C) 29
    D) 30

38) Eight Tar Heels have received ACC Rookie of the Year, which of the following was not one of them?

    A) J.R. Reid
    B) Sam Perkins
    C) Derrick Phelps
    D) Brandan Wright

39) Since the 1972-73 season, the Tar Heels have had how many freshman first-game starters?

    A) 19
    B) 21
    C) 26
    D) 32

40) Since 1964 sixteen Tar Heels have been members (coaches or players) of USA Olympic basketball teams.

    A) True
    B) False

41) Which former Tar Heel won the 2000 NBA Slam Dunk contest?

    A) Vince Carter
    B) Antawn Jamison
    C) Rasheed Wallace
    D) Michael Jordan

42) Which of the following Tar Heels did not play on the 2005 Championship team?

    A) Sean May
    B) Rashad McCants
    C) Jimmy Black
    D) Jawad Williams

43) When the NBA named its All-Time 50 Greatest Players in the late 1990s, how many Tar Heels were selected?

    A) 0
    B) 1
    C) 3
    D) 4

44) All-time, have the Tar Heels had greater than ten players named ACC Player of the Year?

    A) Yes
    B) No

45) What is the Tar Heels' largest margin of victory in an NCAA Tournament game?

    A) 42
    B) 45
    C) 51
    D) 53

46) Tar Heel great Michael Jordan was selected which overall pick in the 1984 NBA Draft?

    A) #1
    B) #2
    C) #3
    D) #4

47) Tar Heel Phil Ford was either 1st or 2nd Team Consensus All-American each of these years except?

    A) 1976
    B) 1977
    C) 1978
    D) 1979

48) The Rick Sharp Award is given to the UNC player who has contributed the most to team practices and behind the scenes.

    A) True
    B) False

Preseason

49) How many NCAA Final Four appearances have the Tar Heels had?

    A) 12
    B) 13
    C) 15
    D) 17

50) In which year did the Tar Heels play their first season of basketball?

    A) 1910
    B) 1911
    C) 1914
    D) 1917

Preseason Tar Heel Cool Fact

1940 and 1941 All-American and a National Player of the Year, George Glamack, known as the "Blind Bomber", used the lines painted on the basketball court as visual reference points for his shots because of his poor eye sight. Using this technique his hook shot became particularly deadly to Tar Heel opponents. Despite this "handicap" George once scored 45 points in a single game and averaged 20.6 points per game in 1941.

Preseason Answer Key

1) C – Dean E. Smith Center (The facility spans 7.5 campus acres and includes 300,000 finished square feet of space.)

2) A – Columbia Blue (Carolina Blue is also sometimes referred to as Sky Blue.)

3) B – Atlantic Coast Conference (UNC was one of seven charter ACC members in 1953.)

4) D – Duke (The Tar Heels and Blue Devils have been waging war on the hardwood since 1920.)

5) C – Chapel Hill (In 1793 construction of the school's first building, known as Old East, was started near the New Hope Chapel Hill Anglican Chapel.)

6) B – Hark The Sound (Based on the tune of Amici, its association with the university dates back to 1897.)

7) A – True (The Tar Heels have an all-time overall record of 1,950-699 [.736].)

8) D – Rameses the Ram (The first live ram was purchased for $25 from a Texas rancher.)

9) B – Four-Corners (Created and perfected by Coach Smith, four-corners helped slow game tempo and some say encouraged the adoption of the shot clock in college basketball.)

10) D – 1986 (The first game played in the Smith Center was on January 18, 1986.)

11) C – 4 (1957, 1982, 1993, & 2005)

12) A – Roy Williams (A 1972 UNC graduate, Coach Williams is beginning his 6th season as head coach.)

13) B – Interlocking "NC" logo (It was changed back to "North Carolina" the following year.)

14) D – Georgetown (Jordan's shot went in with 17 seconds left in regulation giving the Tar Heels a 63-62 lead over the Hoyas.)

15) A – Rams Club (The foundation has been providing financial support to student-athletes since 1938.)

16) A – Yes (This includes Jack Cobb [no # on jersey], Lennie Rosenbluth [#10], Phil Ford [#12], George Glamack [#20], Michael Jordan [#23], Antawn Jamison [#33], and James Worthy [#52].)

17) C – 12 (Boston College, Clemson, Duke, Florida State, Georgia Tech, Maryland, North Carolina, North Carolina State, Miami, Virginia, Virginia Tech, and Wake Forest)

18) D – Tar taken from forests for the English Navy (Although many theories persist, most historians agree the name originated from the tar produced from the early days of the state's history.)

19) B – False (In 1983 Sam Perkins & Michael Jordan were First Team selections, but James Worthy was not.)

20) B – 40 (North Carolina and UCLA are tied with 40 all-
     time NCAA Tournament appearances. Kentucky
     leads all programs with 49.)

21) C – Golden State Warriors (Vince was drafted #5
     overall in 1998.)

22) B – False (Coach Guthridge won 34 of 38 games (.895)
     in the 1998 season, which is currently the Division-
     1 record.)

23) C – Cleveland Cavaliers (#1 pick overall)

24) B – 2 (Eric was selected Second Team Consensus All-
     American two years in a row [1993 and 1994].)

25) A – Kansas (Emporia, KS; Coach Smith was born on
     February 28, 1931.)

26) D – 12 (L. Rosenbluth, B. Cunningham, L. Miller, C.
     Scott, B. Jones, W. Davis, P. Ford, J. Worthy, S.
     Perkins, M. Jordan, B. Daugherty, & A. Jamison)

27) A – True (Including 2007 selections Brandan Wright
     and Reyshawn Terry. No Tar Heels were drafted in
     the 2008 NBA Draft.)

28) D – Antawn Jamison (Although Antawn was the
     recipient of many honors while at UNC, he was
     never named MOP of the NCAA Final Four.)

29) A – 26 (UNC was the outright ACC Champion in 2008.)

30) A – Texas A&M (This record was set in a Midwest
     Second Round game.)

31) D – Duke (Tyler Hansbrough was a unanimous All-ACC First Team selection in 2007-08. He became the 67th Tar Heel to earn the distinction since 1954.)

32) D – Vince Carter (Vince was not a four-year starter at UNC as a result of entering the NBA Draft following his Junior year.)

33) A – True (The Tar Heels have 562 all-time regular-season ACC wins. Duke is second with 469.)

34) C – 8 (Larry Brown, Billy Cunningham, Robert McAdoo, James Worthy, Ben Carnevale, Frank McGuire, Dean Smith and class of 2007 inductee Roy Williams)

35) A – 59 (Tyler Hansbrough is the only active player on the list. UNC leads the nation in this category.)

36) B – Virginia Christian (The Tar Heels won that game in a final score of 42-21.)

37) B – 27 (UNC's consecutive NCAA Tournament appearance record started under Coach Smith and ended under Coach Matt Doherty.)

38) C – Derrick Phelps (Brandan Wright became UNC's most recent ACC Rookie of the Year in 2007.)

39) C – 26 (Brandan Wright was UNC's most recent freshman first-game starter in 2006-07.)

40) A – True (In addition Henrik Rodl played for the German Olympic team in 1992.)

41) A – Vince Carter (Vince defeated Steve Francis and
         Tracy McGrady in the final round of the contest.)

42) C – Jimmy Black (Jimmy played on the 1982
         Championship team.)

43) C – 3 (James Worthy, Michael Jordan, and Billy
         Cunningham)

44) A – Yes (Eleven Tar Heels have won ACC Player of the
         Year, including Tyler Hansbrough for 2007-08.)

45) B – 45 (UNC defeated Rhode Island by 45 points [112-
         67] in an East Second Round game in 1993.)

46) C – #3 (Michael was selected #3 overall by the Chicago
         Bulls following Houston's Akeem Olajuwon and
         Kentucky's Sam Bowie.)

47) D – 1979 (Second Team 1976, First Team 1977, and
         First Team 1978)

48) A – True (The award is voted on by UNC players.)

49) D – 17 (1946, 1957, 1967, 1968, 1969, 1972, 1977,
         1981, 1982, 1991, 1993, 1995, 1997, 1998, 2000,
         2005, and 2008)

50) A – 1910 (The Tar Heels began play on January 27th of
         that year.)

Note: All answers valid as of the end of the 2007-08
season, unless otherwise indicated in the question
itself.

1) In his career, Antawn Jamison was named ACC Player of The Week how many times?

    A) 11
    B) 12
    C) 13
    D) 14

2) Which of the following players did not play for the 1984 USA Olympic Team?

    A) Sam Perkins
    B) James Worthy
    C) Michael Jordan
    D) Steve Alford

3) Joseph Forte received his Consensus All-American selection in which year?

    A) 1998
    B) 1999
    C) 2001
    D) 2003

4) Coach Smith led UNC to how many career victories?

    A) 867
    B) 879
    C) 911
    D) 923

Regular Season *2-Point Questions*

5) How many All-Time NCAA Tournament Games have the Tar Heels played?

    A) 116
    B) 121
    C) 135
    D) 147

6) Which Tar Heel led the team in scoring in 1954-55, 1955-56, and 1956-57?

    A) Joe Quigg
    B) Lennie Rosenbluth
    C) Pete Brennan
    D) Phil Ford

7) How many times was UNC's Dean Smith National Coach of the Year?

    A) 3
    B) 4
    C) 5
    D) 6

8) Which team did UNC beat to get its 1,000th victory?

    A) Hofstra
    B) William & Mary
    C) Maryland
    D) Manhattan

9) The team award given to the Tar Heels' statistically best screener is called?

    A) Mary Frances Andrews Award
    B) Herb C. and Pauline L. Wall Memorial Award
    C) Martha Jordan Award
    D) Oscar Vatz Award

10) How many Tar Heels have been selected CoSIDA First Team Academic All-American?

    A) 5
    B) 6
    C) 8
    D) 9

11) Current Head Coach Roy Williams coached which program prior to North Carolina?

    A) Kansas State
    B) Kentucky
    C) Kansas
    D) Kent State

12) The Tar Heels have attempted 28 three-pointers against two separate teams in NCAA Tournament play.

    A) True
    B) False

Regular Season *2-Point Questions*

13) Which team did the Tar Heels defeat to win the NCAA Championship in 1993?

A) Syracuse
B) Georgetown
C) Illinois
D) Michigan

14) In 2002 the Tar Heels missed the NCAA Tournament for the first time since which year?

A) 1974
B) 1975
C) 1976
D) 1979

15) What number was Bob McAdoo picked in the NBA Draft?

A) #1
B) #2
C) #3
D) #4

16) When ranked #1 or #2 in the *AP* Poll, how many times has UNC played a #1- or #2-ranked Kentucky?

A) 0
B) 1
C) 2
D) 3

17) In which year did the Tar Heels play their last regular-season game in Carmichael Auditorium?

A) 1976
B) 1979
C) 1986
D) 1989

18) What is UNC's all-time highest scoring non-overtime game?

A) 114 points
B) 116 points
C) 117 points
D) 121 points

19) When was the first year UNC played Duke with both schools ranked #1 & #2 in the *AP* Poll?

A) 1957
B) 1973
C) 1994
D) 2001

20) How many times did a Coach Smith-led team win the ACC Tournament?

A) 8
B) 9
C) 12
D) 13

Regular Season *2-Point Questions*

21) Was UNC Head Coach Bill Guthridge ever named National Coach of the Year?

    A) Yes
    B) No

22) In which year did the Tar Heels win their 1,700th game?

    A) 1997
    B) 1998
    C) 1999
    D) 2002

23) Which team did the Tar Heels defeat in the NCAA Championship game in 2005?

    A) Michigan
    B) Kansas
    C) Illinois
    D) Georgetown

24) How many replica jerseys hang in the Smith Center in honor of Tar Heel greats?

    A) 39
    B) 43
    C) 46
    D) 49

Regular Season *2-Point Questions*

25) Which Tar Heel is the only coach to win both an NCAA National Championship and NBA World Championship?

   A) Roy Williams
   B) Ben Carnevale
   C) Frank McGuire
   D) Larry Brown

26) UNC has played in how many games in which they and their opponent were ranked in the top 2 in the *AP* Poll?

   A) 6
   B) 7
   C) 8
   D) 11

27) How many Tar Heels have been named All-American?

   A) 39
   B) 41
   C) 47
   D) 48

28) In which year were the Tar Heels named the National Champions by the Helms Foundation?

   A) 1924
   B) 1937
   C) 1942
   D) 1953

29) On December 17, 1994 the Tar Heels scored 77 points in a half against which team?

A) West Virginia
B) Dartmouth
C) VMI
D) Western Kentucky

30) Which Tar Heel scored 49 points, a team record, in a game against Florida State in 1965?

A) Billy Cunningham
B) Bob Lewis
C) Yogi Poteet
D) Larry Miller

31) Who holds the UNC freshman record for most points scored in a season?

A) Rashad McCants
B) Tyler Hansbrough
C) Joseph Forte
D) J.R. Reid

32) Which Tar Heel holds game, season, and career records for blocked shots?

A) Sam Perkins
B) Brendan Haywood
C) Serge Zwikker
D) Kevin Salvadori

Regular Season *2-Point Questions*

33) How many games has UNC won when they and their opponent are ranked #1 and #2 in the *AP* Poll?

    A) 3
    B) 4
    C) 6
    D) 7

34) How many Tar Heels have gone on to win an NBA World Championship?

    A) 12
    B) 13
    C) 17
    D) 18

35) Which Tar Heel standout was nicknamed "Big Game"?

    A) Kenny Smith
    B) Eric Montross
    C) James Worthy
    D) Frank McGuire

36) What is the official seating capacity of UNC's "Dean Dome"?

    A) 17,525
    B) 18,999
    C) 19,000
    D) 21,750

37) In 1982 did Ralph Sampson set Virginia's team record for most blocked shots versus UNC?

A) Yes
B) No

38) How many points did Michael Jordan score in his first game as a Tar Heel?

A) 3
B) 12
C) 17
D) 23

39) How many points did UNC's Phil Ford have against Duke to set his personal single game scoring record?

A) 29
B) 31
C) 34
D) 38

40) How many NCAA Elite Eight appearances have the Tar Heels had?

A) 16
B) 23
C) 27
D) 32

Regular Season *2-Point Questions*

TAR HEELOLOGY TRIVIA CHALLENGE

41) The Celtics drafted which Tar Heel in the '94 NBA Draft?

    A) Eric Montross
    B) George Lynch
    C) Kenny Smith
    D) J.R. Reid

42) What is the Tar Heels' overall record as a #1 seed in the NCAA Tournament?

    A) 35-15
    B) 41-9
    C) 43-7
    D) 44-6

43) Michael Jordan was honored as Division 1 Player of The Year in which year?

    A) 1982
    B) 1983
    C) 1984
    D) 1985

44) Bob McAdoo was named First Team Consensus All-American in which year?

    A) 1970
    B) 1972
    C) 1976
    D) 1977

45) The Tar Heels do not currently hold the NCAA record for most times defeating an *AP* #1-ranked team.

    A) True
    B) False

46) Wayne Ellington made how many team-leading three-pointers for the Tar Heels in the 2007-08 season?

    A) 59
    B) 63
    C) 78
    D) 84

47) The team award known as the Oscar Vatz Award is given to the statistical leader in which category?

    A) Field-goals Made
    B) Assists
    C) Steals
    D) Rebounds

48) As a team, have the Tar Heels ever shot 80% or higher from the field?

    A) Yes
    B) No

49) Against which team does UNC currently have the highest number of consecutive home victories?

A) Maryland
B) Georgetown
C) Clemson
D) Providence

50) What are the most consecutive weeks the Tar Heels have spent at #1 in the *AP* Poll?

A) 13
B) 15
C) 17
D) 18

Regular Season Tar Heel Cool Fact

Cartwright's Many Firsts – In 1922 Cartwright Carmichael and his brother Billy were the first brothers to play basketball together at UNC. In that same year Cartwright helped the Tar Heels win the Southern Conference's first ever league championship, becoming the first school to be recognized as a league champion in any college sport. Then in 1923 Cartwright became the first Tar Heel to be named First Team All-American for any sport. Finally he led the Tar Heels to their first undefeated season (26-0) and their first National Championship in 1924, as voted retroactively by the Helms Foundation.

Regular Season Answer Key

1) B – 12 (Antawn set this record while at UNC from 1995-98.)

2) B – James Worthy (Michael Jordan and Sam Perkins were the only two UNC players on the 1984 U.S. Olympic team. Steve Alford was on the team but, of course, from Indiana not UNC.)

3) C – 2001 (Forte played at UNC from 1999 to 2001.)

4) B – 879 (Coach Smith had an overall record of 879-254 [.776] in his coaching career.)

5) C – 135 (This includes five NCAA Tournament games played in 2007-08.)

6) B – Lennie Rosenbluth (Lennie averaged 25.5 ppg in 1954-55, 26.7 ppg in 1955-56 & 28.0 ppg in 1956-57.)

7) B – 4 (1977, 1979, 1982, & 1993)

8) C – Maryland (Bob McAdoo helped the Tar Heels win their 1,000th victory on January 29, 1972. The winning score was 73-59.)

9) B – Herb C. and Pauline L. Wall Memorial Award

10) D – 9 (Billy Cunningham [1965], Charlie Scott [1970], Dennis Wuycik [1972], Steve Previs [1972], Brad Hoffman [1975], Ed Stahl [1975], Tommy LaGarde [1975 & 1976], Steve Hale [1986], and Eric Montross [1994])

11) C – Kansas (1989-2003)

12) A – True (Arkansas in a 1995 Final Four game [UNC 68, Arkansas 75] and Texas in a 2004 Atlanta Regional game [UNC 75, Texas 78])

13) D – Michigan (North Carolina 77, Michigan 71)

14) A – 1974 (UNC was 8-20 overall and 4-12 in the ACC.)

15) A – #1 (Bob was the first overall draft pick in 1972 by the Buffalo Braves [Currently known as the NBA's Los Angeles Clippers].)

16) B – 1 (The only time this has happened is on December 26, 1981.)

17) C – 1986 (The Tar Heels were victorious in a score of 90-79 against NC State that game.)

18) D – 121 points (UNC defeated Louisville 121-110 on December 27, 1989.)

19) C – 1994 (February 3, 1994 saw the #2 ranked Tar Heels beat the #1 ranked Blue Devils 89-78.)

20) D – 13 (1967, 1968, 1969, 1972, 1975, 1977, 1979, 1981, 1982, 1989, 1991, 1994, & 1997)

21) A – Yes (Thanks to a 34-4 record and a trip to the Final Four in the 1997-98 season, former Dean Smith assistant Guthridge was named National Coach of the Year.)

22) B – 1998 (This happened on February 11, 1998 in a game against Virginia.)

23) C – Illinois (On April 4, 2005 the Tar Heels defeated Illinois 75-70 to win the National Championship.)

24) B – 43 (The jerseys are replicas of those worn by each honored Tar Heel standout.)

25) D – Larry Brown (Coach Brown led Kansas to an NCAA National Championship in 1988 & the Detroit Pistons to an NBA World Championship in 2004.)

26) B – 7 (The most recent was on April 4, 2005 when the #2 ranked Tar Heels played #1 ranked Illinois.)

27) D – 48 (Tyler Hansbrough and Brandan Wright were added to the list of UNC All-American selections following the 2006-07 season. Tyler received Consensus First Team honors again for the 2007-08 season.)

28) A – 1924 (The Tar Heels went 26-0 that season.)

29) C – VMI (At the end of the first half UNC led 77-42.)

30) B – Bob Lewis (December 16, 1965)

31) C – Joseph Forte (600 points in the 1999-2000 season)

32) B – Brendan Haywood (Brendan's team records are as follows: Game, 10; Season, 120; and Career 304.)

33) D – 7 (The Tar Heels are 7-0 in games in which they and their opponent hold the top two *AP* Poll rankings.)

34) B – 13 (These 13 players have won a combined total 28 NBA World Championships.)

35) C – James Worthy (Accomplishments like the MOP of
      the 1992 NCAA Championship Game earned
      James this nickname.)

36) D – 21,750 (As of 2000, seating adjustments brought
      seating capacity to 21,750.)

37) B – No (Ralph set the record for most rebounds [19] for
      Virginia against UNC.)

38) B – 12 (UNC defeated Kansas 74-67 in that game.)

39) C – 34 (Phil hit 13-19 field goals en route to 34 points.)

40) B – 23 (1941, 1946, 1957, 1967, 1968, 1969, 1972,
      1977, 1981, 1982, 1983, 1985, 1987, 1988, 1991,
      1993, 1995, 1997, 1998, 2000, 2005, 2007, & 2008)

41) A – Eric Montross (Selected #9 overall by the Celtics)

42) B – 41-9 (The Tar Heels have entered the NCAA
      Tournament 12 times as a #1 seed [1979, 1982,
      1984, 1987, 1991, 1993, 1994, 1997, 1998, 2005,
      2007, & 2008.)

43) C – 1984 (Michael averaged 19.6 ppg, 5.3 rpg, 2.1 apg,
      and 1.6 spg to earn himself Player of the Year for
      the 1983-84 season.)

44) B – 1972 (He was also named to the All-Regional
      Team and All-Final Four Team for the NCAA
      Tournament that season.)

45) B – False (The Tar Heels do currently hold this record,
      with 12 all-time victories over *AP* #1-ranked teams.)

46) C – 78 (Wayne was 78 of 195 [.400] from three-point land in 2007-08.)

47) D – Rebounds (This award is sometimes also referred to as the Benjamin and Oscar Vatz Award.)

48) B – No (However the Tar Heels were 49 of 62 [.790] versus Loyola Marymount on March 19, 1988.)

49) C – Clemson (The Tar Heels have totaled 52 consecutive victories in home games from 1926-2008 versus the Tigers.)

50) B – 15 (From December 6, 1983 to March 13, 1984)

Note: All answers valid as of the end of the 2007-08 season, unless otherwise indicated in the question itself.

1) The Tar Heels' record for most consecutive 20-win seasons was set over how many seasons?

   A) 25 seasons
   B) 28 seasons
   C) 30 seasons
   D) 31 seasons

2) In 1959 York Larese hit 100% of how many free throw attempts against arch rival Duke to set a school record?

   A) 21
   B) 22
   C) 23
   D) 24

3) Which Tar Heel holds the school record for most assists in a four-year career?

   A) Phil Ford
   B) Vince Carter
   C) Ed Cota
   D) Hubert Davis

4) In which season was Michael Jordan UNC team captain?

   A) 1981-82
   B) 1982-83
   C) 1983-84
   D) He was never a permanent team captain

5) In each of his four years at UNC, Scott Williams led the team in which statistical category?

A) Most Charges Drawn
B) Most Steals
C) Most Blocked Shots
D) Most Defensive Rebounds

6) The Tar Heels set their record for highest FG percentage in a half by shooting 16 of 17 against which team?

A) Virginia
B) Syracuse
C) Clemson
D) Boston College

7) What is the Tar Heel's Most Inspirational Player Award known as?

A) Foy Roberson Award
B) Carmichael-Cobb Award
C) Jimmie Dempsey Award
D) Burgess McSwain Award

8) In 2000, what did Brendan Haywood lead the nation in?

A) Minutes Played
B) Field-goal Percentage
C) Three-point Percentage
D) Blocking Fouls Drawn

9) Which team is noted for having hit twenty-one three-point field goals against North Carolina?

A) Duke
B) Maryland
C) Georgia Tech
D) Kentucky

10) Which Tar Heel performed the "Dunk of Death" over French Center Frederic Weis in the 2000 Olympics?

A) Brendan Haywood
B) Vince Carter
C) Eric Montross
D) Brad Daugherty

11) What is the biggest jump UNC has made from being unranked to ranked (*AP* top 25) from the previous week?

A) 4th
B) 10th
C) 12th
D) 21st

12) In 1985 which Tar Heel hit a team record thirteen of thirteen consecutive field goals against UCLA?

A) Kenny Smith
B) Brad Daugherty
C) Kevin Madden
D) Jeff Lebo

13) What is the lowest *AP* ranking from which the Tar Heels have risen to the #1 ranking?

A) #18
B) #20
C) #22
D) #25

14) Who was selected for more First and Second Team Consensus All-American honors?

A) James Worthy
B) Michael Jordan
C) Sam Perkins
D) J.R. Reid

15) Which team attempted the most three-point FGs against UNC in an NCAA Tournament game?

A) Duke
B) Illinois
C) Iowa
D) Old Dominion

16) When did Antawn Jamison earn Division 1 Player of The Year?

A) 1995
B) 1996
C) 1997
D) 1998

Conference Tournament *3-Point Questions*

17) How many NCAA Sweet 16 appearances have the Tar Heels had?

   A) 22
   B) 24
   C) 26
   D) 28

18) Sam Perkins was only the second freshman to win ACC Tournament MVP in which year?

   A) 1981
   B) 1982
   C) 1983
   D) 1984

19) Did Maryland hand the Tar Heels their first loss in the Smith Center?

   A) Yes
   B) No

20) How many wins did it take Coach Smith to break Adolph Rupp's then all-time coaching record in 1997?

   A) 603
   B) 707
   C) 877
   D) 921

21) In December of 2003 which opponent had the most points ever allowed (119) by the Tar Heels?

A) Wake Forest
B) Georgia Tech
C) Air Force
D) Texas

22) What jersey number does Tyler Hansbrough wear?

A) 50
B) 52
C) 54
D) 55

23) What is Indiana's and UNC's shared NCAA record for most victories in a perfect season?

A) 30
B) 31
C) 32
D) 35

24) Coach Smith was not the first ACC coach to win 700 games.

A) True
B) False

25) Who was the first opponent the Tar Heels played in the Smith Center on January 18, 1986?

A) Arkansas
B) Baylor
C) Clemson
D) Duke

26) Which legendary Tar Heel was called the Kangaroo Kid?

A) Lennie Rosenbluth
B) Phil Ford
C) Billy Cunningham
D) Bob Lewis

27) What season did UNC win its 1,800th game?

A) 2001
B) 2003
C) 2004
D) 2005

28) UNC set a team record for most rebounds (64) in an NCAA Tournament game against which Ivy League school in 1967?

A) Harvard
B) Yale
C) Princeton
D) Columbia

29) Which Tar Heel holds the school record for highest field-goal percentage in a season?

    A) Rick Fox
    B) Bobby Jones
    C) Brendan Haywood
    D) Rasheed Wallace

30) What is UNC's single season team record for most points scored?

    A) 3,257
    B) 3,272
    C) 3,331
    D) 3,454

31) In how many games in the 2007-08 season did the Tar Heels score 100 or more points?

    A) 7
    B) 8
    C) 10
    D) 11

32) Which Tar Heel holds the team record for most consecutive three-pointers made?

    A) Jason Capel
    B) Shammond Williams
    C) Dante Calabria
    D) Raymond Felton

33) Rusty Clark grabbed 30 rebounds to set a Tar Heel school record against Maryland in which year?

A) 1968
B) 1969
C) 1970
D) 1971

34) Which Tar Heel played the most total career games?

A) Pete Chilcutt
B) George Lynch
C) Rick Fox
D) Brendan Haywood

35) What is the highest number of blocked shots an opposing player has had against the Tar Heels?

A) 7
B) 8
C) 10
D) 16

36) Each of the following Tar Heels averaged a double-double in their careers, except?

A) Billy Cunningham
B) Sean May
C) Lennie Rosenbluth
D) Mitch Kupchak

37) Jeff Lebo set a Tar Heel team record by doing what 41 consecutive times?

A) Making free throws
B) Making field goals
C) Making three-pointers
D) Scoring double digits

38) In 1981 UNC & Indiana played an NCAA Championship game that was nearly postponed due to which event?

A) Tropical Storm
B) Assassination attempt on Ronald Reagan
C) Mechanical troubles with their bus
D) Referee Strike

39) What is UNC's team record for fewest turnovers in a single game?

A) 0
B) 1
C) 2
D) 3

40) Who is the only Tar Heel to attempt more than 200 three-pointers in two separate seasons?

A) Shammond Williams
B) Hubert Davis
C) Donald Williams
D) Kenny Smith

41) Have seven or more Tar Heels ever averaged double digit scoring in the same season?

A) Yes
B) No

42) Which Tar Heel is the only player in NCAA history with greater than 1,000 points, 1,000 assists, and 500 rebounds in a career?

A) Ed Cota
B) Billy Cunningham
C) Jason Capel
D) James Worthy

43) How many points per game did Michael Jordan average while at UNC?

A) 11.9
B) 13.2
C) 17.7
D) 21.4

44) "Black Sunday" in March of 1979 saw The Tar Heels lose along with which team?

A) Clemson
B) NC State
C) Duke
D) Penn

45) Tar Heel standout Antawn Jamison was originally drafted by which team?

A) New York Knicks
B) Toronto Raptors
C) New Jersey Nets
D) Golden State Warriors

46) Which of the following schools has spent more weeks at #1 on the *AP* Poll than the Tar Heels?

A) Kentucky
B) Cincinnati
C) UCLA
D) Kansas

47) Against which opponent do the Tar Heels currently have the most consecutive victories?

A) Florida State
B) Virginia
C) Duke
D) VMI

48) What is the highest number of blocked shots the Tar Heels have recorded in a single game?

A) 18
B) 19
C) 20
D) 22

49) In his four years (1980-84) with the Tar Heels, which 6'10" player had 2,133 points and 1,167 rebounds?

A) James Worthy
B) Sam Perkins
C) Al Wood
D) Matt Dougherty

50) Billy Cunningham received which award, as voted by his teammates, for three consecutive years?

A) Martha Jordan Award
B) Mary Frances Andrews Award
C) Foy Roberson Award
D) Most Valuable Player

Conference Tournament
Tar Heel Cool Fact

A lot can be accomplished in a college basketball career. Take for instance becoming the only junior-college transfer to ever receive a basketball scholarship from Dean Smith, averaging 19.5 points per game and 10.1 rebounds per game, winning ACC regular-season and tournament championships, making a Final Four appearance, and becoming an All-ACC & ACC Tournament MVP. Capping it all off by becoming the first player to ever leave UNC early for the NBA Draft and later being inducted into the Naismith Basketball Hall of Fame. Not a bad career at all considering Robert McAdoo accomplished all of this in just one season at North Carolina.

Conference Tournament Answer Key

1) D – 31 seasons (1971 to 2001)

2) A – 21 (York Larese hit 21 of 21 free throws against Duke on December 29, 1959.)

3) C – Ed Cota (From 1996-2000 Ed had 1,030 assists in 138 career games with UNC.)

4) D – He was never a permanent team captain (1981-82 UNC team captains were Jeb Barlow, Jimmy Black, and Chris Brust; 1982-83 team captain was Jim Braddock; and 1983-84 team captains were Matt Doherty, Cecil Exum, and Sam Perkins.)

5) C – Most Blocked Shots (In 1986-87 Scott Williams, J.R. Reed, and Dave Popson each had 27 blocked shots to lead the team. In 1987-88 Scott led UNC outright with 43 blocked shots. He then had 50 and 41 team-leading blocked shots in 1988-89 and 1989-90 respectively.)

6) A – Virginia (On January 7, 1978 UNC was .941 from the field in the 2nd half of play. This is both the team and NCAA record.)

7) A – Foy Roberson Award (The award is named after a former player who made the ultimate sacrifice to the U.S.A. in World War II. Players and coaches vote on the award annually.)

8) B – Field-goal Percentage (That season Brendan hit 191 field goals out of 274 [69.7%].)

9) D – Kentucky (On December 27, 1989 Kentucky shot 21 three-pointers against the Tar Heels.)

10) B – Vince Carter (Carter scissored over 7'2" Frederic Weis's head for what French journalists would later dub "le dunk de la mort", which translates to "the dunk of death".)

11) C – 12th (This happened in 2002 between the weeks of November 26th and December 3rd.)

12) B – Brad Daugherty (The UCLA game was on November 24, 1985. In UNC's next game vs. Iona he hit 3 more consecutive shots to set the team's multi-game consecutive field-goals record [16].)

13) A – #18 (This occurred from January 4 to February 1, 1983.)

14) C – Sam Perkins (1982 Second Team; 1983 First Team; and 1984 First Team)

15) B – Illinois (Illinois attempted 40 three-pointers against the Tar Heels in the 2005 NCAA Final.)

16) D – 1998 (Antawn joined Michael Jordan as the only Tar Heels to ever be voted Naismith College Player of The Year.)

17) D – 28 (UNC defeated Washington State 68-47 in its 28th Sweet 16 appearance in the 2008 NCAA Tournament.)

18) A – 1981 (In 1975 Carolina's own Phil Ford was the first freshman to ever win the honor.)

19) A – Yes (Maryland defeated UNC 77-72 in overtime on February 20, 1986. It was UNC's only home loss the inaugural season of the Smith Center.)

20) C – 877 (This happened on March 15, 1997 in a victory against Colorado in the NCAA Tournament.)

21) A – Wake Forest (This occurred in a triple-overtime game on December 20, 2003 that saw the Tar Heels lose 114-119.)

22) A – 50 (The same number he wore at Poplar Bluff High School, Poplar Bluff, MO. His number is set to be honored at the conclusion of his UNC career.)

23) C – 32 (UNC's perfect season was 1956-57.)

24) B – False (Coach Smith set this record on January 9, 1991 against Maryland.)

25) D – Duke (Fittingly the Tar Heels defeated arch rival Duke in a score of 95-92.)

26) C – Billy Cunningham (A small forward, Billy was known for his exceptional leaping ability.)

27) B – 2003 (The Tar Heels achieved this mark with a 68-65 victory vs. Connecticut on January 18, 2003.)

28) C – Princeton (March 17, 1967 in a game played at Cole Field House in College Park, Maryland)

29) C – Brendan Haywood (In 36 games Brendan hit 191 out of 274 field-goal attempts [.697].)

30) D – 3,454 (This team record was set in the 2007-08 season. The previous record of 3,331 was achieved in 1988-89.)

31) B – 8 (UNC scored 107 vs. Iona, 110 vs. South Carolina State, 106 at Penn, 105 vs. UC Santa Barbara, 106 vs. Nevada, 103 vs. Clemson, 113 vs. Mount St. Mary's, and 108 vs. Arkansas.)

32) D – Raymond Felton (Raymond had 12 straight three-pointers in the 2004-05 season.)

33) A – 1968 (Rusty set this enduring mark on February 21, 1968.)

34) D – Brendan Haywood (Brendan played in 141 games while at UNC from 1997-2001.)

35) C – 10 (Dikembe Mutumbo blocked 10 Tar Heel shots on December 7, 1989.)

36) D – Mitch Kupchak (Mitch averaged a double-double in the 1974-1975 and 1975-1976 seasons, but not over his entire career.)

37) A – Making free throws (Jeff's consecutive free throws were in games spanning from January 3 to March 12, 1989.)

38) B – Assassination attempt on Ronald Reagan (The game was played less than eight hours after the attempted assassination.)

39) C – 2 (This happened in a game against Fairfield on March 13, 1997.)

40) A – Shammond Williams (Shammond attempted 227 in
the 1996-97 season & 215 in the 1997-98 season.)

41) B – No (Although J.R. Reid, Kevin Madden, Steve
Bucknall, Jeff Lebo, Rick Fox, and Scott Williams
all did in the 1988-89 season.)

42) A – Ed Cota (Ed's career stats in these categories are
1,261 points, 1,030 assists, and 517 rebounds.)

43) C – 17.7 (Michael averaged 13.5 as a Freshman, 20.0
as a Sophomore, and 19.6 as a Junior.)

44) C – Duke (Black Sunday saw the Tar Heels lose to
Penn 72-71 and Duke lose to St. John's.)

45) B – Toronto Raptors (Golden State immediately traded
cash and Vince Carter for the rights to Antawn.)

46) C – UCLA (UNC has spent 96 weeks at #1 compared
to the Bruins' 134 weeks. Duke also has more
weeks at #1 [110].)

47) D – VMI (33 consecutive wins in games from 1922-97)

48) A – 18 (December 20, 1985 vs. Stanford)

49) B – Sam Perkins (Sam accomplished this feat in 135
career games with the Tar Heels.)

50) D – Most Valuable Player (1962-63 through 1964-65)

Note: All answers valid as of the end of the 2007-08
season, unless otherwise indicated in the question
itself.

Championship Game   *4-Point Questions*

1) Which famous Tar Heel jumped center against Wilt Chamberlain in the 1959 Championship Game?

    A) Tommy Kearns
    B) Danny Lotz
    C) Lee Shaffer
    D) York Larese

2) Michael Jordan led the ACC in scoring in which of his three years as a Tar Heel?

    A) Freshman
    B) Sophomore
    C) Junior
    D) Michael Jordan never led the ACC in scoring

3) How many all-time NCAA Tournament games has UNC won?

    A) 96
    B) 98
    C) 100
    D) 104

4) In 1986 UNC's Brad Daugherty led the nation in which statistic?

    A) Free Throws Made
    B) Assists
    C) Free Throw Attempts
    D) Field-goal Percentage

5) What is the Tar Heels' team record for most assists in a single game?

    A) 29
    B) 34
    C) 37
    D) 41

6) In the 1956-57 & 1957-58 seasons UNC had its longest all-time winning streak with how many consecutive wins?

    A) 32
    B) 34
    C) 37
    D) 40

7) In 1998 UNC beat which #1 ranked team by 24 points?

    A) Virginia
    B) UCLA
    C) St. John
    D) Duke

8) In which year was J.R. Reid selected First Team Consensus All-American?

    A) 1986
    B) 1988
    C) 1990
    D) 1991

9) In 1923-24 which Tar Heel coach set a record for the Best Career Start by Percentage?

    A) Norman Shepard
    B) Winton Green
    C) Harry Woodburn Chase
    D) Frank McGuire

10) What is the name of the award originally given for the Tar Heels' overall statistical leader in a season?

    A) Burgess McSwain Award
    B) Jimmie Dempsey Award
    C) Butch Bennett Award
    D) Rick Sharp Award

11) Which of the following has never beaten UNC in the NCAA Tournament?

    A) Notre Dame
    B) Dartmouth
    C) Arkansas
    D) Florida

12) How many 3-pointers did Shammond Williams hit to set a UNC record for 3-pointers in an NCAA Tournament Game?

    A) 5
    B) 6
    C) 7
    D) 8

13) What are the fewest points the Tar Heels scored in a game coached by Dean Smith?

   A) 37
   B) 38
   C) 42
   D) 45

14) Which Tar Heel holds the team's career-points record?

   A) Lennie Rosenbluth
   B) Sam Perkins
   C) Phil Ford
   D) Al Wood

15) What is UNC's highest team scoring average for a season?

   A) 89.4 ppg
   B) 91.3 ppg
   C) 96.1 ppg
   D) 97.8 ppg

16) Which Tar Heel played in the most games won by UNC in his college career?

   A) Lennie Rosenbluth
   B) King Rice
   C) Eric Montross
   D) Sam Perkins

17) How many documented (not necessarily official) triple-doubles have Tar Heel players accomplished?

    A) 3
    B) 4
    C) 5
    D) 6

18) Which Tar Heel holds all of the school's records in the category of double-digit rebounding games?

    A) Bobby Jones
    B) Larry Miller
    C) Bud Maddie
    D) Billy Cunningham

19) Which of the following players was the point guard for 2 Tar Heel squads that went undefeated in ACC action?

    A) Ed Cota
    B) Jerry Stackhouse
    C) Kenny Smith
    D) Derrick Phelps

20) Have the Tar Heels ever allowed an opposing player to score 48 or more points against them in a single game?

    A) Yes
    B) No

21) How many times was Coach Smith voted ACC Coach of the Year?

    A) 6
    B) 7
    C) 8
    D) 9

22) What are the most overtime periods in a single game the Tar Heels have played in?

    A) 3
    B) 4
    C) 5
    D) 6

23) Have any Tar Heels ever played 40 games in a single season?

    A) Yes
    B) No

24) In which city did Coach Smith coach his final game for UNC?

    A) Indianapolis, IN
    B) Chapel Hill, NC
    C) Charlotte, NC
    D) Durham, NC

25) Which event caused UNC to reschedule a game in 1991?

    A) Blizzard
    B) Outbreak of the Gulf War
    C) Presidential Inauguration Celebration
    D) Iraqi Invasion of Kuwait

26) Against which team did UNC set a team record for most steals in an NCAA Tournament game in 1976?

    A) New Mexico
    B) Penn State
    C) Gonzaga
    D) Alabama

27) Which of the following Tar Heels won the team's Outstanding Senior Award?

    A) Sam Perkins
    B) Ed Cota
    C) Brad Daugherty
    D) All of the above

28) Coach Roy Williams holds several Division 1 coaching records in which of the following categories?

    A) Number of Games Won
    B) Technical Fouls
    C) Total Games Coached
    D) Fastest to Landmark Victories

29) In which two cities have the Tar Heels won the greatest number of NCAA Tournament games?

    A) East Rutherford, NJ & Indianapolis, IN
    B) Charlotte, NC & Syracuse, NY
    C) Anaheim, CA & Denver, CO
    D) Tampa, FL & Washington, DC

30) In the 1995 NBA Draft, two Tar Heels were selected consecutively as the third and fourth overall picks.

    A) True
    B) False

31) How many seasons was Bill Guthridge head coach at UNC?

    A) 1
    B) 2
    C) 3
    D) 4

32) The Tar Heels attempted 91 field goals in an NCAA Tournament game against which team?

    A) Michigan
    B) Ohio State
    C) Notre Dame
    D) USC

Championship Game

4-Point Questions

TAR HEELOLOGY TRIVIA CHALLENGE

33) In which year was UNC the first school ever to have four lottery selections in the NBA Draft?

- A) 1984
- B) 1994
- C) 2005
- D) 2006

34) In which year was UNC's first NCAA Tournament Game?

- A) 1931
- B) 1937
- C) 1939
- D) 1941

35) What are the most rebounds a Tar Heel has ever grabbed in a single game in the Smith Center?

- A) 17
- B) 24
- C) 27
- D) 34

36) Who was not one of the starters in 2002 when the Tar Heels started three freshmen for the first time ever?

- A) Rashad McCants
- B) Raymond Felton
- C) Sean May
- D) Jawad Williams

NORTH CAROLINA TAR HEELS BASKETBALL

68

37) Who holds the team record for most points & most rebounds in a single NCAA Tournament game?

A) Charles Scott
B) Robert McAdoo
C) Lennie Rosenbluth
D) Al Wood

38) Which Tar Heel set the Smith Center record for most points scored?

A) Antawn Jamison
B) Ed Cota
C) Brendan Haywood
D) Tyler Hansbrough

39) Which of the following is not a UNC assistant coach?

A) Steve Robinson
B) Joe Holladay
C) C.B. McGrath
D) Jerod Haase

40) Which Tar Heel standout suffered a leg injury 12 seconds into a national semifinal game in 1995?

A) Jerry Stackhouse
B) Rasheed Wallace
C) Ed Cota
D) None of the above

41) Who was the Tar Heels' leading scorer in the 1982 NCAA Championship game versus Georgetown?

  A) Sam Perkins
  B) James Worthy
  C) Michael Jordan
  D) Buzz Peterson

42) How many steals did Derrick Phelps need to set UNC's single game steals record?

  A) 7
  B) 9
  C) 10
  D) 11

43) What is Raymond Felton's school record for most assists by a Tar Heel in a single game?

  A) 18
  B) 19
  C) 21
  D) 23

44) What is UNC's team record for most points scored in a single game?

  A) 124
  B) 129
  C) 131
  D) 142

45) In a 1979 game against Duke, UNC did not attempt a single field goal until how many minutes into the game?

A) 7:01
B) 7:28
C) 9:03
D) 12:25

46) What is the Tar Heels' overall record against a #1 seed in the NCAA Tournament?

A) 4-6
B) 5-5
C) 7-3
D) 8-2

47) In the 1991 NBA Draft, what was the highest position a Tar Heel was selected?

A) #3
B) #8
C) #24
D) #27

48) Which Tar Heel led the team in scoring in the 1993 NCAA Championship Game?

A) Eric Montross
B) George Lynch
C) Donald Williams
D) Brian Reese

49) Coach Smith is ranked second for the Fastest to 800 Wins behind which other coach?

    A)   Adolph Rupp
    B)   Bob Knight
    C)   Jerry Tarkanian
    D)   Mike Krzyzewski

50) How many total Consensus First-Team All-American selections have the Tar Heels had?

    A)   12
    B)   13
    C)   17
    D)   19

Championship Game Tar Heel Cool Fact

In 1965, Coach Smith's fourth year at UNC, following four consecutive losses, dissatisfied students decided to hang Coach Smith in effigy for the team to see upon their return to campus. The rest, as they say, is history. Dean Smith went on to win 879 games – second most in NCAA Division 1 basketball history, coached the Tar Heels to thirteen ACC Tournament Championships, eleven Final Fours, and two National Championships. In his career he was voted ACC Coach of the Year eight times. He was inducted into the North Carolina Hall of Fame in 1981, the Naismith Memorial Basketball Hall of Fame in 1983, and the National Collegiate Basketball Hall of Fame in 2006. In 1986 Coach Smith's likeness would be hung once again, but this time it was in the dedication of the Dean E. Smith Center on UNC's campus. It is unclear whether or not any of the angry students from 1965 were in attendance in Chapel Hill on this night.

Championship Game Answer Key

1) A – Tommy Kearns (Most notably because Kearns was just under 6' in height.)

2) C – Junior (Michael Jordan led the ACC in scoring that year with a 19.6 scoring average.)

3) A – 96 (UNC added 4 more victories to their total by defeating Mount St. Mary's, Arkansas, Washington Sate, and Louisville in the 2008 NCAA Tournament.)

4) D – Field-goal Percentage (That season Brad hit 284 of 438 field goals for a .648 average.)

5) D – 41 (UNC set this team record against Manhattan on December 27, 1985 in the Orange Bowl Classic [UNC 129, Manhattan 45].)

6) C – 37 (The streak began on December 4, 1956 vs. Furman [94-66] and ended the following season on December 21, 1957 vs. West Virginia [64-75].)

7) D – Duke (#2 North Carolina defeated #1 Duke at home by 24 points [97-73] on February 5, 1998.)

8) B – 1988 (J.R. averaged 18 points per game and 8.9 rebounds per game for the Tar Heels that season.)

9) A – Norman Shepard (Coach Shepard had a Division-1 record start of 23-0 [.1000] in the 1923-24 season.)

10) B – Jimmie Dempsey Award (Beginning in 2006 this award is now given to the most improved player on the team.)

11) A – Notre Dame (The Tar Heels are 3-0 versus the Irish in NCAA Tournament play.)

12) B – 6 (The record was set in Hartford, Connecticut in an East Regional Second Round game on March 14, 1998 against UNC Charlotte.)

13) D – 45 (February 12, 1997 The Tar Heels beat NC State in a score of 45-44.)

14) C – Phil Ford (Phil scored 2,290 career points while at UNC from 1974-78. Sam Perkins has the second most with 2,145 points from 1980-84.)

15) B – 91.3 (This record was set in the 1986-87 season when UNC had 3,285 total points in 36 games played.)

16) D – Sam Perkins (Sam played in 115 total Tar Heel victories from 1980-84.)

17) A – 3 (Brendan Haywood [18 points, 14 rebounds, & 10 blocks], Jason Capel [16 points, 11 rebounds, & 10 assists], and Billy Cunningham [33 points, 16 rebounds, & 11 assists as reported by the *Charlotte Observer* in 1965] are the only Tar Heel players reported to have triple-doubles.)

18) D – Billy Cunningham (He holds this distinction for most games rebounding in double figures in a season [22], in a career [61], and consecutive games rebounding in double figures [40].)

19) C – Kenny Smith (This happened in the 1983-84 & 1986-87 seasons. In both seasons UNC was a perfect 14-0 in ACC games.)

20) A – Yes (Dick Groat from Duke scored 48 points against the Tar Heels in a game on Feb. 29, 1952.)

21) C – 8 (1967, 1968, 1971, 1976, 1977, 1979, 1988, & 1993)

22) B – 4 (This took place in a game against Tulane on February 14, 1976.)

23) B – No (Although Tyler Hansbrough, Wayne Ellington, Danny Green, Deon Thompson, and Marcus Ginyard all played in 39 games in the 2007-08 season.)

24) A – Indianapolis, IN (Coach Smith's final game as Tar Heel Head Coach was on March 29, 1997 versus Arizona in the NCAA Final Four [UNC 58, Arizona 66].)

25) B – Outbreak of the Gulf War (The game originally scheduled for January 16, 1991 had to be played on February 7, 1991 due to Operation Desert Storm.)

26) D – Alabama (UNC had 16 Steals in a Mideast First
    Round game in 1976 versus Alabama. Although
    the Tar Heels would lose that game 64-79.)

27) D – All of the above (Sam Perkins, 1983-84; Ed Cota
    1999-2000; and Brad Daugherty, 1985-86)

28) A – Number of Games Won (Best Career Starts by
    Wins and Most Wins in 9 to 17 Seasons)

29) B – Charlotte, NC & Syracuse, NY (The Tar Heels have
    a 9-0 and 7-1 NCAA Tournament record in these
    two cities respectively, including two victories in
    Charlotte in the 2008 tournament.)

30) A – True (Jerry Stackhouse was selected third overall
    by Philadelphia & Rasheed Wallace was selected
    fourth overall by Washington.)

31) C – 3 (Coach Guthridge retired in June of 2000 after
    three years as head coach.)

32) B – Ohio State (1946 Eastern Regional Final played at
    Madison Square Garden [UNC 60, OSU 57])

33) C – 2005 (Marvin Williams was the 2nd overall pick by
    the Atlanta Hawks, Raymond Felton was the 5th
    overall pick by the Charlotte Bobcats, Sean May
    was the 13th overall pick by the Charlotte Bobcats,
    and Rashad McCants was the 14th overall pick by
    the Minnesota Timberwolves.)

34) D – 1941 (UNC was defeated 20-26 by Pittsburgh on March 21, 1941 in their first-ever NCAA Tournament game. The following day they lost again by a score of 59-60 to Dartmouth.)

35) B – 24 (Sean May set this school record versus Duke on March 6, 2005.)

36) D – Jawad Williams (Rashad McCants, Raymond Felton, & Sean May all started in a victory over Penn State [85-55].)

37) C – Lennie Rosenbluth (39 points against Canisius in 1957 and 19 rebounds against Yale in 1957.)

38) D – Tyler Hansbrough (Tyler set this record with 40 points in a game against Georgia Tech on February 15, 2006.)

39) D – Jerod Haase (Jerod is currently the Director of Basketball Operations, not an assistant coach.)

40) A – Jerry Stackhouse (The loss of Stackhouse contributed to Arkansas's defeating North Carolina that game in a final score of 68-75.)

41) B – James Worthy (James had 28 points on 13-17 from the field and 2-7 from the free throw line.)

42) B – 9 (This record was set on February 2, 1992 against Georgia Tech.)

43) A – 18 (Versus George Mason on December 7, 2003)

44) B – 129 (The Tar Heels have scored 129 points on two occasions, once on December 17, 1994 against VMI [129-89] and once against Manhattan on December 27, 1985 [129-45].)

45) D – 12:25 (Duke led UNC 7-0 heading into the locker room at half time thanks to UNC's delay strategy and missed shots. Duke went on to win the game 47-40 after both teams coincidentally scored 40 points in the second half of play.)

46) C – 7-3 (Kansas defeated UNC 84-68 in the 2008 Final Four to hand the Tar Heels their 3rd all-time loss to a #1 seed in the tournament.)

47) C – #24 (Rick Fox was selected 24th overall by the Boston Celtics. Just three picks later [27th pick], Pete Chilcutt was taken by the Sacramento Kings.)

48) C – Donald Williams (Donald led the team in scoring that night with 25 points on 8-12 field goals and 5-7 free throws.)

49) A – Adolph Rupp (Coach Rupp won his 800th after 972 games and Coach Smith won his after 1,029.)

50) D – 19 (14 individual players on 19 occasions)

Note: All answers valid as of the end of the 2007-08 season, unless otherwise indicated in the question itself.

Overtime Bonus *4-Point Questions*

1) What is UNC's all-time longest winning streak in the Smith Center?

    A) 25 games
    B) 28 games
    C) 34 games
    D) 37 games

2) Who was the last Tar Heel CoSIDA Academic All-American?

    A) J.R. Reid
    B) Steve Hale
    C) Eric Montross
    D) None of the above

3) What is UNC Head Coach Roy Williams's career winning-percentage?

    A) .721
    B) .792
    C) .807
    D) .843

4) UNC's Best Free Throw Percentage Award, also known as the Martha Jordan Award, is named for Michael Jordan's sister?

    A) True
    B) False

Overtime Bonus *4-Point Questions*

5) How many NCAA Championship Game appearances have the Tar Heels had?

  A) 4
  B) 5
  C) 6
  D) 8

6) What are the most points Tyler Hansbrough scored in a game in UNC's 2007-08 season?

  A) 32
  B) 36
  C) 39
  D) 42

7) Antawn Jamison played which position while at UNC?

  A) Guard
  B) Forward
  C) Center
  D) Split time 50/50 between Center and Forward

8) How many NCAA Tournament games have the Tar Heels lost when scoring 90 or more points in a game?

  A) 0
  B) 2
  C) 4
  D) 5

Overtime Bonus *4-Point Questions*

9) In 1989 the Charlotte Hornets drafted which Tar Heel as the fifth overall pick in the NBA Draft?

    A) Kenny Smith
    B) J.R. Reid
    C) Joe Wolf
    D) Jeff Lebo

10) Who is the only Tar Heel to receive unanimous All-ACC honors in both their freshman and sophomore years?

    A) Phil Ford
    B) Billy Cunningham
    C) Michael Jordan
    D) Tyler Hansbrough

Overtime Bonus Answer Key

1) A – 25 games (From March 4, 1992 to February 12, 1994 UNC won 25 consecutive games at home.)

2) C – Eric Montross (Eric received this honor in 1994.)

3) C – .807 (In 20 years coaching, Coach Williams holds an all-time coaching record of 560-134.)

4) B – False (Michael's sisters are Deloris E. Jordan & Roslyn M. Jordan and there is no relation to the award's namesake.)

5) D – 8 (1946, 1957, 1968, 1977, 1981, 1982, 1993, & 2005)

6) C – 39 (Tyler was 11-16 from the floor and 17-19 from the free throw line versus Clemson on February 10, 2008.)

7) B – Forward

8) A – 0 (The Tar Heels are 11-0 when they score 90-99 points & 9-0 when scoring 100 or more points.)

9) B – J.R. Reid (J.R. was the only Tar Heel drafted in that year's NBA Draft.)

10) D – Tyler Hansbrough (2006 & 2007)

Note: All answers valid as of the end of the 2007-08 season, unless otherwise indicated in the question itself.

Player / Team Score Sheet

TAR HEELOLOGY TRIVIA CHALLENGE

Name:

Preseason		Regular Season		Conference Tournament		Championship Game		Overtime	
1	26	1	26	1	26	1	26	1	
2	27	2	27	2	27	2	27	2	
3	28	3	28	3	28	3	28	3	
4	29	4	29	4	29	4	29	4	
5	30	5	30	5	30	5	30	5	
6	31	6	31	6	31	6	31	6	
7	32	7	32	7	32	7	32	7	
8	33	8	33	8	33	8	33	8	
9	34	9	34	9	34	9	34	9	
10	35	10	35	10	35	10	35	10	
11	36	11	36	11	36	11	36		
12	37	12	37	12	37	12	37		
13	38	13	38	13	38	13	38		
14	39	14	39	14	39	14	39		
15	40	15	40	15	40	15	40		
16	41	16	41	16	41	16	41		
17	42	17	42	17	42	17	42		
18	43	18	43	18	43	18	43		
19	44	19	44	19	44	19	44		
20	45	20	45	20	45	20	45		
21	46	21	46	21	46	21	46		
22	47	22	47	22	47	22	47		
23	48	23	48	23	48	23	48		
24	49	24	49	24	49	24	49		
25	50	25	50	25	50	25	50		

___x 1 =____   ___x 2 =____   ___x 3 =____   ___x 4 =____   ___x 4 =____

Multiply total number correct by point value/quarter to calculate totals for each quarter.

Add total of all quarters below.

Total Points:_____

Thank you for playing Tar Heelology Trivia Challenge.
Additional score sheets are available at:
www.TriviaGameBooks.com

85

Player / Team Score Sheet

TAR HEELOLOGY TRIVIA CHALLENGE

Name:_____

Preseason		Regular Season		Conference Tournament		Championship Game		Overtime
1	26	1	26	1	26	1	26	1
2	27	2	27	2	27	2	27	2
3	28	3	28	3	28	3	28	3
4	29	4	29	4	29	4	29	4
5	30	5	30	5	30	5	30	5
6	31	6	31	6	31	6	31	6
7	32	7	32	7	32	7	32	7
8	33	8	33	8	33	8	33	8
9	34	9	34	9	34	9	34	9
10	35	10	35	10	35	10	35	10
11	36	11	36	11	36	11	36	
12	37	12	37	12	37	12	37	
13	38	13	38	13	38	13	38	
14	39	14	39	14	39	14	39	
15	40	15	40	15	40	15	40	
16	41	16	41	16	41	16	41	
17	42	17	42	17	42	17	42	
18	43	18	43	18	43	18	43	
19	44	19	44	19	44	19	44	
20	45	20	45	20	45	20	45	
21	46	21	46	21	46	21	46	
22	47	22	47	22	47	22	47	
23	48	23	48	23	48	23	48	
24	49	24	49	24	49	24	49	
25	50	25	50	25	50	25	50	
__ x 1 =__		__ x 2 =__		__ x 3 =__		__ x 4 =__		__ x 4 =__

Multiply total number correct by point value/quarter to calculate totals for each quarter.

Add total of all quarters below.

Total Points:_____

Thank you for playing Tar Heelology Trivia Challenge.
Additional score sheets are available at:
www.TriviaGameBooks.com